EXPLORING MINDFULNESS

Twenty-six weekly sessions to breathe mindfulness into your life

PAUL RICHES

CONTENTS

❧ I ❧

INTRODUCTION

This is the first book in a four-part series that takes you on an incremental journey to explore, expand, enhance and embed mindfulness in your daily experience. Each book is organised in twenty-six weekly theme-based sessions, so, if you cover one session a week, you have enough for six months self-development and exploration.

The sessions have been developed, delivered and refined over six years within both private and public sector organisations in face-to-face, audio conference and online formats.

Each session is supported by guided audio practices to play or download, which work online as well as on a smartphone. Simple instructions on how to access the audios that accompany this book are covered in the Guided practices section at the end of the book.

These sessions blend secular mindfulness, evolutionary psychology, relevant scientific and social research together with challenges with our contemporary lifestyles.

The main focus is on improving well-being and performance

at work as well as in your personal life, by helping you to achieve the following learning outcomes:

- Understand what mindfulness is and how it makes a difference
- Experience how mindfulness can improve your well-being and performance
- Be familiar with using a range of mindfulness techniques
- Understand the causes, and be better able to manage, stress, anxiety and low-mood
- Intentionally focus your attention
- Notice when your mind wanders
- Be able to discriminate between automatic thoughts that are useful, positive and nurturing and those that are not useful, negative and depleting
- Appreciate the difference between reacting and responding in various situations
- Experience the benefits of using mindfulness attitudes like acceptance, kindness, gratitude and curiosity
- Use and benefit from informal mindfulness practices like mindful eating, walking and listening
- Be more able to observe your own thoughts, emotions and sensations
- Establish a regular daily meditation practice
- Be more skilful in communications and relationships

Benefits of mindfulness

As well as the workplace, mindfulness is making a difference within health, education, sports, prisons and the military. Studies in the workplace show that practicing mindfulness delivers physical, psychological, and social outcomes that translate into business benefits like improved performance, productivity and decision-making.

On a personal level, people who regularly practice mindfulness arc happier, healthier and experience less anxiety, stress and low-mood. There's also a stronger connection with life, as well as a rich appreciation about what it means to be human and alive.

How to use this book

Of course, it's up to you how you use this book, but to get the most out of it, see if you can commit to setting aside around thirty minutes on one day of the week, maybe a Sunday morning or Monday evening, somewhere comfortable and where you can remain undisturbed.

The session chapters have been ordered alphabetically by theme, as it's assumed that the book does not have to be read from beginning to end. So, depending on what's going on in your life, maybe pick a session that most resonates you at the time, and see what difference that makes.

To play the related guided audio, you'll need a smartphone, tablet or computer with Internet access that can play sound at a reasonable quality. See the Guided practices section at the end of this book to find out how to access these audio resources.

EXPLORING MINDFULNESS

Mindfulness has been around for over two and a half thousand years and can be found, in one form or another, in all major religions. The present-day secular practice of mindfulness was developed in the Stress Reduction Clinic at University of Massachusetts Medical School in the 1990s. This approach has since been adapted to make a difference within health, education, the workplace, professional sports, the military and in prisons.

Mindfulness is not some special mystical state to you have to discover, it's something we're all familiar with but maybe did not have a name for before. Remember the last time you were completely involved in an activity, where you felt a sense of ease and your attention was simply absorbed in whatever you were doing. For instance, this could have been painting a picture, baking a loaf of bread, or gazing in awe at a wonderful sunset. All of these experiences have one thing in common - your attention is in the here-and-now and not drifting off in thought.

For instance, you're not mulling over whether you offended

someone yesterday, worrying about a report you have to produce, or holiday plans. Your attention is connected with the flowing moment of experience, the activity, your senses and other people involved.

Natural selection has equipped us with an amazing brain that's built to analyse, plan, problem-solve and create. The upside is that when we're "thinking on purpose", these abilities are immensely powerful. In that last 500 years, we've developed the scientific method, split the atom, walked on the moon, unraveled DNA and built the Internet. The downside is that our brains are so powerful, they sometimes take over our attention with a type of thinking that's not so deliberate. This is when our mind wanders. Recent research found that, on average, our attention drifts off in thought, away from the present activity, as much as 48% of the time. Typically our mind wanders into an imagined future, or mulls over past memories. When engage on this mental "time traveling", we disconnect from the present moment.

The research also found that people reported being less happy when mind wandering. The question is, apart from the present moment, when else can you actually experience happiness and the richness of being alive? It's no surprise that this form of overthinking contributes to stress, anxiety, and depression.

When we practice mindfulness, we develop the awareness to notice, and the attention skills to disconnect from automatic thinking, when it's not useful, and come back to the present moment. All you need to do is bring our attention to your body and senses. Like the phrase "come to your senses", your body and senses are only ever in the present.

This awareness provides a greater clarity on what's going on internally, as well as in the external world in any particular moment. Without awareness, we tend to grasp pleasant feelings and avoid unpleasant ones. So, for example, an email appears at work chasing up a deadline on a project you're leading. As you read the email, you notice feelings of anxiety and stress and some negative thoughts bubbling up. Rather than push these unpleasant feelings away, you take a moment to acknowledge them. Maybe saying internally "Oh, there's some anxiety, stress and some negative thoughts about myself and the sender. That's to be expected with the pressure of this deadline. The project's okay and I don't need to act out these feelings". After acknowledging what's going on, you take an aware breath and exhale slowly and respond effectively to the email.

Mindfulness works with thoughts, emotions and body sensations, as well as how they interact. For instance, say that a difficult customer makes you feel annoyed. Angry thoughts arise and you may start to feel tense and hot in your body. Through practicing mindfulness you develop the skills to notice the feeling of annoyance as it arises from an objective distance. Rather than immediately identifying with the feeling, you may have the thought "Oh, there's some frustration. Although this customer is being really difficult, I don't need to act on how I feel". Within this aware space, you have greater freedom to respond appropriately, rather than reacting automatically.

Seventy-thousand years ago we survived and thrived as hunter-gatherers. The industrial revolution began just 257 years ago and arguably, the digital age in the last 40. There's little physiological difference between how we're configured today and the bodies of our ancient ancestors who foraged for food and watched out for danger. So, there's a misalignment between our hunter-gather biology and the challenges and opportunities we encounter in the modern world. So it's no wonder we sometimes experience stress, anxiety and low mood. Through developing our attention and awareness, combined with other skills and attitudes like acceptance, openness, curiosity, and kindness, we begin to close the gap and explore what it is to be human.

☙ 3 ❧

ACCEPTANCE

One simple way to define mindfulness is that it's about working skilfully with present-moment experience. The skilful bit is about bringing a set of skills and attitudes to your experience. Practising mindfulness is not just about learning the theory; like playing the piano, or riding a bike, it's all about embodying and refining the skills and attitudes through experience. Acceptance is an important one of these.

We live in an increasingly turbulent world with globalisation, climate change and new technology driving change across the political, economic and cultural landscape, which affects all of us on an individual level. There are also smaller events that are closer to home, from the uncertainty about your job to losing all the edits on a report you've been writing, or making good progress on the motorway only to get trapped in a three-lane car park for hours. Life does not always go the way we hope. Feelings of frustration, low mood and anxiety can quickly arise. Our mind gets busy with negative thoughts about who's to blame; we catastrophise; our self-worth takes a dive and our body tenses up with the stress.

In his book, "The Power of Now" Eckhart Tolle provides three useful options for difficult situations: leave it, change it, or accept it totally. There are some situations you can just walk away from and others you can improve by changing something. Then there are situations where neither of these is an option, where you just need to embrace reality as it is and accept it.

Acceptance means consciously allowing things to be as they already are. Although this seems simple and obvious, it's not always as easy as it sounds.

Some of the things that make this difficult include:

- How we interpret the world at the time through our thoughts, beliefs and perceptions, which can be useful to help make sense of reality but are not reality itself. Thoughts about, "How annoying the rain is" are very far from the physical phenomena of rainfall.
- We all want life to go smoothly and get our needs met, but there are some things we can influence and many others that we can do nothing about. For instance, we could check the traffic and take public transport if there is heavy traffic, but if we're already driving and there's an accident ahead there may be little we can do.
- A related third factor is that we often take things too personally when many things are impersonal and would have happened whether we existed or not.

Acceptance means turning towards a difficulty rather than habitually avoiding or resisting it. For example, if someone irritates you, rather than reacting, just stay with the feeling of irritation. Connect with the sensations in your body and notice any thoughts that emerge. Are you taking this situation too personally? Are you being overly critical or judge-mental? How much of this is to do with you rather than with them? Of course, there are some people who will always irri-tate you, but by accepting their behaviour and not taking things personally you open the possibility of relating to the person differently, in a kinder and more compassionate way.

Acceptance does not mean you've lost a battle or become a victim. It's about finding an easier path through a difficulty, by embracing and working with reality as it is. Resistance and avoidance are generally automatic and habitual ways of coping that may seem to work at the time, but often make things more complicated and difficult in the long-term. By accepting "what is" you create the space and freedom to act.

So, the next time you're faced with an unwanted or difficult situation, take a few moments to pause, allowing the situation to be just as it is, connecting into the present moment, aware of your body and breath, maybe noticing the impulse to react, then responding with the most appropriate option, which may well be to completely accept the situation as it is.

SUGGESTED WEEKLY PRACTICE

- Notice when you feel the impulse to react automatically and see what happens if you choose to accept whatever the situation presents instead.
- If you find yourself in a queue in a shop or traffic, try letting go of feeling impatient, accepting the situation and notice if anything changes.
- Notice if you tend to personalise things, when they are in fact impersonal.

❦ 4 ❦

ALERTNESS

Anyone who explores mindfulness soon discovers that although the theory is relatively straight-forward, a bit like learning to play the piano, mastering the practice is not easy. Apart from consistent daily practice, one of the key ingredients is the level of alertness we bring to our practice. So, if you're meditating for ten minutes on your breath and feel tired and have low energy, you're much more likely to drift off in thought away from the intention of the exercise, or even fall asleep.

When our awareness and energy drops, a part of our mind is well rehearsed to take over with automatic thoughts, like a running commentary, or narrative at the edge of awareness. When our level of conscious awareness drops, the brain picks up that there's not much going on and switches into mind-wandering mode. In fact, neuroscientists have recently identified part of the brain called the default mode network, which becomes active when nothing much is happening. Like a radio chattering away in the background, our mind is wandering and we're only half aware. Research shows that our minds wander away from the current task around 48% of the time, which is half of our waking lives. Of course, mind-wandering can be really useful; we may be in the shower when the solution to a complex problem we've been struggling with pops into our heads, or we have creative thoughts about a project we're working on. But there's a downside to mentally drifting, which is that automatic thoughts tend to be negative. Typically, these will be negative automatic thoughts that are self-critical and limiting. So being able to notice when our mind wanders is an important skill. A useful tip is to ask yourself, "Where is my attention now?" and see what you discover.

One of the fundamental steps in practising mindfulness is to notice that your attention has wandered away from what you were doing. This is most obvious when we are following our breath with our attention. One moment we're completely with it, the next we're rehearsing what we're going to say in a meeting later in the day. We go from one thought to another until we realise that we intended to focus on our breath. The next step is to acknowledge where our attention went, then gently return our attention to the breath. One challenge is that the transition from following the breath to being off in thought is so fast that we barely notice. Another is that our attention wandered because our level of awareness dropped. In other words, we were not alert at the time. So, our level of alertness is an important inner resource. The word "alert" comes from the Italian "all'erta" meaning on the watch, or on the look-out. Alertness is the level of energy in our attention, our wakefulness and watchfulness - our level of conscious awareness.

One way of describing a mindful state is that it's calm and alert. Although this sounds like an oxymoron, what it means is that all agitation and restless movement is relatively settled and that we're awake and watchful. If it helps, imagine an experienced motorcyclist, who is calm and relaxed, but at the same time completely alert to hazards from the road and other drivers. Interestingly, motorcyclists often say that they enjoy riding because they're so in-the-moment with their experience.

There are many benefits to cultivating mindfulness, including increased performance, wellbeing and reduced anxiety and stress. Being aware of your level of alertness and boosting it when you need to, can make a real difference to realising these benefits.

~

Suggested weekly practice

- Check-in with yourself during the day to notice your level of alertness. If it's low, take a few fuller in-breaths to bring energy into your body. If this is not making a difference go somewhere where you can move around and exercise a little to get your body moving and energy flowing. For instance, take the stairs rather than the lift.
- Notice what makes you less alert, and when. You could try keeping a brief journal on your level of alertness to discover patterns. Do you need more sleep? A bit more exercise? Maybe more fresh fruit and vegetables, or lighter lunches? See what works for you.
- Get into the habit of asking, "Where is my attention now?" to gain insights, while also bring yourself back to and alert and aware state.

ALLOWING

In our busy and demanding work and home lives we can accumulate mental and emotional agitation and noise, which is often carried into the next activity and accumulates over the rest of the day. Challenging situations can cause stress as well as unpleasant emotions like anger, anxiety, or sadness to emerge. Sometimes we act out on the strong emotions, reacting unskilfully, upsetting ourselves and others. At other times, our impulse is to defend ourselves from these unwanted feelings, by ignoring and avoiding them altogether. Unnoticed and unacknowledged, the feelings remain in the background, triggering negative automatic thoughts, which end up amplifying and re-activating the emotion in a potentially endless loop. When negative emotions remain unacknowledged, we can often feel limited and depleted within ourselves and isolated from those around us.

So why is working with emotions like fear and anger difficult and what can we do about it?

Over hundreds of millions of years, the brain evolved to spot threats in the environment and take action to survive. Then a few millions of years ago, the mammalian brain developed a way of learning to anticipate threats. As humans, we have both systems for noticing and reacting to threats; the flexible, slow and deliberate thinking of the neocortex that works from the top-down, together with the much faster, automatic emotions, which work from the bottom-up from the brain stem and amygdala.

Most of our senses are wired through the brain stem, which sits below the amygdala. When the amygdala reacts to a perceived threat in our environment, it triggers the fight-or-flight response so that the body is ready for action. While this is very useful if you suddenly come across a lion, going into a stress response as you open what looks like an ominous-looking email, is not so helpful. Our body contracts; muscles tighten and stress hormones like adrenalin and cortisol are released.

Although emotions evolved before language and thoughts, they are useful and vital in at least three ways: firstly, they tell us that something needs attention; they communicate how we feel to others and thirdly, they drive us to act.

As humans, although we may acknowledge the power of emotions, we tend to be dominated by thoughts, so process things from the top-down. With mindfulness we take a different approach, which is to notice thoughts, but also become more aware of what happens from the bottom-up, through the body. So, when that ominous email arrives, before running off in worrying thoughts about losing your job, try tuning into your body, where you may notice the body contracting and stress and anger starting to rise. You can then respond more skilfully by being more open and accepting to what the email contains; allowing the experience to simply be as it is, without wanting to change things, or for anything to be different.

Acknowledging and allowing emotions to be "just as they are", involves breaking free of old reactive habits and takes a bit of trust and courage. Turning towards emotions like fear can seem like a huge unsurmountable wall, yet from the other side we may find that it's just a single brick that we can easily step over. Just like the mighty Wizard of Oz, who turned out to be a harmless old man speaking into a machine behind a curtain.

Allowing means:

- Being present to what's going on in your body
- Coming out of the "virtual reality" of thoughts and directly connecting with your body
- Bringing kindness, openness and curiosity to your experience
- Not wanting to change or fix what you experience
- Befriending painful and unpleasant emotions like anger, sadness and anxiety
- Applying less friction and flowing with your experience

Feelings and emotions are an important, untapped resource, which can provide an early insight into what's going on. Turning towards and acknowledging our feelings and emotions helps reduce stress and allows emotions to flow and dissolve, rather than become stuck in our body. By learning to allow painful and unpleasant feelings and emotions we can live with greater ease, as well as improve our health and wellbeing.

Suggested weekly practice

- Try asking, "what feelings am I not allowing?" and see what arises.
- Notice your impulse to want to change your experience. Instead when you notice and unconformable emotion, try turning towards what you feel, including where the feeling resonates in the body and explore what happens with curiosity.
- Bring kindness, openness and self-compassion to what you feel and experience.

﹩ 6 ﹩

BEGINNER'S MIND

W hen we were children we had an attitude of openness and wonder as we experienced things for the first time, before preconceptions and beliefs in our mind started attenuating and filtering out the dazzling world around us. The term "Beginner's Mind" originally comes from Zen Buddhism and Japanese martial arts and is about bringing an attitude of openness and flexibility to what's in front of you in the moment. Whether this is a person, an object, a problem to be solved, or a decision to be made. Even though you may be an expert, beginner's mind means putting aside existing habits, preconceptions and opinions when approaching a subject - as if you were a beginner. There's a saying in Zen practice:

> *"In the beginner's mind there are many possibilities, in the expert's mind there are few."*

Our brains have evolved to be very efficient; for instance, they help us filter out redundant information, which saves cognitive resources by not fully processing things that we've come across before. A good example is that our brains only fully process the central part of our visual field, while the periphery is left as a blur, as it's not necessarily important. Another is that we often don't fully look at familiar people we see every day. Although these shortcuts, filters and assumptions are useful, they can limit our openness to new possibilities as well as create a barrier for connecting with the real world around us. So, during a typical day, we can easily go around encountering people and situations with little appreciation or awareness as our brain filters out "what we already know".

Research psychologists discovered the Einstellung effect, which happens when we encounter problems that are similar to ones we've already experienced. The effect occurs when we become fixed on a past solution, which may not always be the best or most appropriate answer. For instance, expert chess players will spot a solution and then search for better alternatives, but tracking their eye movements showed that they were biased towards the first one they thought of. So, even experts are prone to the Einstellung effect, which in the case of medical misdiagnosis, can literally mean life or death.

As we learn from experience we develop powerful mental short-cuts. Although relying on previous experience may be useful, there is a downside. It's been said that there are two types of experts, those who rely on experience alone, and those who use experience together with an awareness of the limits of their expertise.

An open beginner's mind allows us to be receptive to new possibilities and prevents us from getting stuck in a rut of our own habits and limitations. This means being curious, inquisitive and open.

It's interesting that letting go of our habitual way of

perceiving the world means reversing some of the efficiencies our brain developed through evolution. This does not mean that we ignore useful knowledge and learning. We make the best of what we know but are also aware of, and flexibly open, to new possibilities.

So how do you cultivate beginner's mind in your daily life?

You can start by observing that no moment of experience is the same as any other. Each is unique and contains distinct possibilities. For example, try using beginner's mind the next time you take a shower, exploring the sensations of the water against your skin, the smell and texture of the soap you're using, appreciating the pleasure of the warm water – as if for the first time.

You can also try using beginner's mind to explore solutions to problems as they arise – without immediately jumping to the most obvious, first or past solution.

The next time you see somebody who's familiar to you, try asking yourself, "Who's here now?" Are you seeing this person through fresh eyes, as she or he really is – a full and complex human being just like you - or is your perception limited through the filter of your own beliefs and assumptions, almost like seeing the person as a cardboard cut-out? Beginner's mind means bringing openness to new possibilities with other people and the world around us, which allows us to fully connect with and properly acknowledge the rich complexity of reality.

Suggested weekly practice

- When you next see someone you know really well,

like your spouse, try asking yourself, "Who's in front of me now?" and see what difference that makes.

- If you have a problem, try using beginner's mind to search for solutions beyond the most obvious.
- Have fun seeing the world around you, opening up fresh perspectives and new ways of seeing beyond assumptions and habits.

❧ 7 ☙

BEING IN YOUR BODY

The human body is a fantastically complex, self-sustaining organism that has something like 10 trillion cells and 11 different systems all working together to keep us active, healthy and alive.

Our body is something we take for granted but completely rely on every day for walking, talking, thinking, breathing and many other things. Apart from aches and pains, for much of the time, our body remains outside of our awareness.

For 90% of human history, it would have been normal to see your body as part of nature, no different from the plants and animals that you encountered. This makes sense, as all the cells in our body are built and replenished from food from the earth, which, at one level, makes us no different from all the other living organisms on the planet.

Yet in the modern western world, we've ended up with a distorted and limited relationship with our own bodies. Many adults feel deep down that their body's not good enough; it's too fat; too short, too old or ugly. The way we view our body is strongly influenced by what's promoted as attractive by society and the media. It's unfortunate that what's held up as attractive tends to be extreme, rather than normal. For example, female models tend to be very young, very thin and tall.

These comparative judgements can be very damaging. It's a sad fact that few people feel completely comfortable with their body; we could go through the whole of our life and never feel completely at home in our body. This will remain until we change our relationship with our body, together with the thoughts and feelings we have about it.

Imagine for a moment that your body was your favourite pet or a child, then consider how you relate to it. Is this with kindness, connection, care and compassion? When compared with the bodies of our hunter-gatherer ancestors, sometimes our poor bodies have to endure long periods of stress, are not properly exercised, are over-fed unhealthy food and emotionally neglected – not a way we would be happy treating a dog.

Like heads on sticks, as human beings in the 21st Century, we tend to spend most of our attention lost in thought or pulled into external distractions like smartphone apps, with little awareness of connection with our body. Practising mindfulness is about coming back to the body and senses, which are always in the present moment, even though our attention may be elsewhere. We can assume that our ancient ancestors were much better connected with their bodies, as research on hunter-gathers who exist today shows that they see themselves as very much part of nature. In our "civilised world" we've gone through a long phase of being lost in thought, as we've drifted and abstracted away from our connection with nature. Perhaps the next phase is being consciously aware of both the positive and negative power of thought, but also connecting our body and nature, with that power.

Being in the body is about building a kind, caring and compassionate relationship with your body; feeling grateful for and appreciating the miraculous body you have. Being in the body also means bringing more of your body into awareness, rather than off in thought in your mind. Although thoughts can be very useful, they take us away from the here-and-now of being in the body. Being in the body means that you're more connected and at-one with your experience. So, if you're walking along the street being in your body, you can enjoy the pleasure and delight of your body walking for you, keeping balance and making progress, all without any conscious need to control the movements, which is something most of us take for granted.

One of the best ways to get in touch your body is to open your awareness to your physical sensations. Rather than the normal way we see the body from the outside in, by becoming aware of physical sensations we gain a sense of what the body feels like from the inside out, which is quite a different experience. We tend to normally filter things that happen all the time, but when you tune into physical sensations you're reclaiming your body in that moment, making yourself more vital and alive.

SUGGESTED WEEKLY PRACTICE

- Intentionally nurturing a kinder, caring and more compassionate relationship with your body; feeling grateful for and appreciating the miraculous body you have.
- Reviewing how well you treat your body with

nutritious food, regular exercise and a proper night's sleep.

- Remembering to tune into your body during the day to bring yourself into the present moment and also notice what tightness and tension you may have accumulated that you can now consciously relax and release now that you are more aware of it.

❦ 8 ❧

BREATH

I t's commonly said that fish are oblivious to the water they live in. Our ancestors may have experienced a similar lack of awareness about the earth's atmosphere, as it was not until the 1770's that some of its components, including oxygen, were discovered.

Breath is one of those comforting certainties of life; if you're alive your body will be breathing. We can survive roughly three weeks without food, three days without water, but only three minutes without oxygen. Given how critical breathing is, it's a great example of one of those things we take for granted every day.

The average human takes about sixteen breaths a minute and over 20,000 breathes a day; consuming a septillion, that's a number with 42 zeros, of oxygen molecules. The good news is that most of our breaths are managed for us automatically by the brain stem. This is the early "reptilian" part of our brain that's the result of millions of years of evolution, which is just as well if you consider what you'd have to do without it.

Our breath changes with physical demands, like walking up a long staircase. It also changes with how we feel so it's no surprise that there's a strong link between breath and emotion. When we're stressed, anxious, angry, or sad our breathing can be affected. Fast and shallower breathing is triggered by the adrenal gland as it kicks us into fight-or-flight mode, which also increases stress hormones like adrenalin and cortisol. Higher levels of cortisol impair learning and memory, lower immune function, increase blood pressure, the risk of heart disease, mental illness and lower life expectancy; clearly something to avoid if we can.

The good news is that simply practising intentional and aware breathing can switch off the fight-or-flight response and switch on the relaxation response of the parasympathetic nervous system, which reverses the physiological effects of stress. Intentional breathing is when we take control of our breath to increase energy, or calm and relax the body, mind and emotions.

The more common way of practising mindfully with the breath is to allow the body and brain stem to do its work; breathing naturally without interfering. If it helps, imagine peacefully watching a pet breathing.

As well as an indicator of what's going on for us physically and emotionally, we can also use the breath as an anchor into the present moment. Focussing on the breath decouples our attention from our thoughts into a grounded connection with our body, which is only ever in the present moment. It takes us out of mulling over past memories and imagined futures to focus our attention on this unique moment.

So if you find yourself feeling agitated, stressed, or anxious, gently bring your awareness to your breath for a few moments. Noticing your body breathing for you if you can, while letting all the movement of mind and emotions gently settle and come to rest.

Breath is fundamental to life; we can't live without it. Learning to be more aware of the breath and using it as a tool to release any agitation or stress brings you into the present moment and makes a real difference to your health, wellbeing and performance.

SUGGESTED WEEKLY PRACTICE

- Using your breath as a stabilising anchor into the present moment, away from automatic thoughts, settling mental agitation and calming emotional turbulence.
- Noticing and appreciating how the breath brings moment-to-moment energy into the body.
- If you notice that you are drifting during meditation, take a series of deeper, intentional breaths to raise your levels of alertness.

❦ 9 ❦

CALM AND ALERT

A re you a lark or an owl? Some of us are "larks" and have more energy in the morning, while "owls" have more energy later in the day. Along with many other creatures, including mammals, birds and insects, we're subject to circadian rhythms, which govern our alertness and sleep cycles during the day. If you've ever suffered from jet lag, you'll have experienced just how powerful this regular cycle is, as your body remains tuned to the previous time zone, until it adjusts to the new location. Although there are individual differences, the average person is most energised in the hours before midday; then energy dips around mid-afternoon and peaks again around 6pm.

As well as the ebb and flow of our sleep-wake cycle, we also have different intensities of activity, agitation and tension going on in our minds, emotions and body that interfere with our performance and wellbeing during the day. For instance, if you had a misunderstanding with your spouse or partner before leaving the house in the morning, the feelings can "niggle away" in the background during the work-meeting.

We also take on stress and anxiety from the burden of activity, emails and other demands that accumulate at work. Although some level of positive stress can be motivating, like working towards a deadline, negative stress from being overburdened adds to our level of agitation, diminishes our ability to perform at our best and can lead to more serious health issues in the long term.

So during a typical workday there are many challenges on our energy as well as our level of agitation and stress. When we practise being mindful, the optimum state is to be both calm and alert. Although this may sound unrealistic, like being asleep and hyperactive at the same time, it's an achievable state that anyone can experience.

With consistent practice, we are able to settle mental agitation and restlessness, so the mind becomes more like the clear, reflective surface of a lake, rather than the choppy waves of the sea, blown by the wind and tides. Being alert means being awake and responsive to whatever arises in our experience. When calm and alert, it makes sense that the mind is able to respond faster and more effectively than when it's full of agitation and noise.

The same goes for emotions and the body. By acknowledging emotions and allowing them to dissolve in their own time, we no longer hold onto them in the body and reduce the amount of thoughts triggered by the emotion. Noticing tightness, tension and stress in the body, we are able to intentionally let go, relax and release what may otherwise remain unnoticed in the background. Although there can be purely physical causes, a significant amount of tension in the body holds unresolved feelings that we have yet to process. The most effective way of processing these feelings is not by thinking what they might be about, but by working bottom-up with your body using an approach like Focusing. Developed in the 1970s. the Focusing process works from with the body, rather than mind, to understand and resolve held feelings and emotions.

We can practise being calm and alert every time we meditate. During meditation we often use the breath to settle any mental and emotional agitation or restlessness. We can also use the breath to increase alertness. When meditating, we can sometimes drift off and feel a bit sleepy and disengaged. If you notice this happening, the best thing to do is take a few quick full and deep breaths to raise your energy and alertness, as you re-engage with the intention of the mediation.

There's a poetic saying by a 13th Century Zen philosopher called Dogen, who wrote:

"Body like the mountain, heart like the ocean, mind like the sky".

There are many challenges with life today, but by bringing ourselves into a state where we're calm and alert, we can take on the various tasks of the day with greater focus, flexibility and ease.

≈

Suggested weekly practice

- Get into the habit of checking how calm and alert you are during the day.
- If you find that you not calm, improve your calmness by closing your eyes and taking a deep in-breath and slowly breathing out with the word "calm" resonating

through your body all the way down to the soles of
your feet.

- If you feel that your alertness has dropped, especially
during meditation, take in a few deeper and
energising breaths and notice your body becoming
re-energised.

CONNECTING

Keeping in touch with friends and those we love is an important part of life, whether this is through meeting up, phone calls, or social media. We connect at some level with everyone we interact with, whether this is a friend, close relative, or a complete stranger serving us in a shop or cafe. As human beings, we've evolved as social animals and have a deep need to feel connected and in touch with others.

More fundamentally, we need to feel connected with the rich experience that life offers. This is why putting a prisoner in an isolation cell is such an extreme punishment. Even in our daily lives, when we lose connection, we can experience feeling a bit isolated, separate, limited or alone.

So why is it that we sometimes lose connection with other people and also with our experience?

Albert Einstein answers this very eloquently:

> "A human being is a part of the whole called by us "Universe", a part limited in time and space. He experiences

himself, his thoughts and feelings as something separated from the rest, a kind of optical delusion of his consciousness. This delusion is a kind of prison for us, restricting us to our personal desires and to affection for a few persons nearest to us. Our task must be to free ourselves from this prison by widening our circle of compassion to embrace all living creatures and the whole of nature in its beauty."

Our awareness and attention are capable of being connected with our mind, emotions, body and senses in the present moment. With practice, it's possible to hold our attention on what someone's saying, while noticing and acknowledging thoughts and emotions as they arise, without losing connection. Instead, what typically happens in conversation is that we become distracted by our thoughts, as we rehearse our own response and wait impatiently for our turn to speak.

As Einstein pointed out, it's easy to get lost in our own ideas, desires and impulses; seeing other people as separate from us, and ourselves as unique individuals. We can reverse this paradox by recognising that everyone we encounter shares a common humanity. And by being non-judging, open and compassionate, we can make a big difference to the quality of our relationships. Even complete strangers have similar feelings with highs and lows, hopes and fears and experience a complex inner life just like our own. The realisation that we're all connected reframes who we think we are: no longer a single, isolated unit at the centre of your own separate world.

Our experience is enabled by conscious awareness and mediated through our attention. We like to think that we are masters of our own attention. The truth is that our attention often unconsciously switches to something else. As we identify with where our attention goes as "Me", we often claim retrospectively that this was our choice, when in fact our attention was pulled-away externally, or internally by thoughts, emotions or physical sensations. The most common form, when our mind wanders off in thought, happens almost half of our waking lives. So, being aware of where your attention is in any moment is fundamental to the quality of our experience.

To be in touch and connected is not just about paying attention; it's about appreciating the amazing richness and vitality that life and human relationships have to offer. Dropping out of thoughts and bringing your attention and awareness back to your body and senses in the present moment is the real key.

SUGGESTED WEEKLY PRACTICE

- Without being inappropriate, explore how you can connect with strangers, maybe having a friendly chat with someone in a lift or shop and smiling with your eyes with people who meet your eye.
- Bringing generosity, empathy and compassion to people who you encounter during the day.
- Explore how richly connected you are with your surroundings; the sights, sounds, tastes, smells and touch.
- Bringing the thought to mind, "This is it! This is the only time I can experience being alive". You maybe doing something really mundane, but life is not a rehearsal.

11

CURIOSITY

Mindfulness is about working skilfully with present-moment experience. Curiosity is an important one of these skills that helps us notice, gain insight and explore the subtle richness of experience.

The word derives from the Latin "curiosus", meaning to be careful, inquiring and diligent. Using curiosity, we can reveal what lies behind the assumptions we apply to reality that may otherwise remain hidden and filtered out of our awareness. For instance, that our thoughts and identity are often bound together.

This type of curiosity is not about problem-solving and analysing with the mind, it's about using your attention and awareness to really explore what you experience. This can include a thought, an emotion, a feeling, impulse, behaviour, taste, sound, or a physical sensation in the body. Curiosity is a useful tool for moving beyond what our mind 'knows', to a more connected, vivid and raw experience of reality.

Mindful curiosity works with direct experience that cuts

through held assumptions, expectations and judgements, as well as the impulse to resist, avoid or change what we're experiencing. When we're curious, we're also practising accepting and allowing things to be as they already are.

One practical example is using curiosity to relieve pain. Imagine that you have a slight headache, for instance, rather than ruminating about how awful it is, try approaching the discomfort with curiosity. You can explore the actual physical sensations by asking yourself:

- Does it feel warm or cold?
- How far does the area extend?
- What does the pain actually feel like?

Using curiosity in this way begins to change the nature of your relationship with your experience, so may well change how you feel about it. Interestingly, there's a growing body of research evidence that practising mindfulness can help relieve physical pain.

Curiosity means asking questions and challenging assumptions about your experience, for instance:

- Noticing that one moment you were aware and the next moment you're drifting off in thought. How did this happen, why did you not notice the transition?
- Using curiosity the next time you feel angry. Instead of acting on it, or entertaining angry thoughts, acknowledge and allow the emotion so it can take its natural course and see what happens

Playful exploration, discovery, insight and learning are all involved when we practise curiosity. By being curious we're more engaged with the world around us, which provides a sense of meaning. Cultivating curiosity enriches our experience, breaks through our self-imposed blind-spots and helps us to become more skilful with our present-moment experience, which improves our wellbeing as well as performance.

SUGGESTED WEEKLY PRACTICE

- Tasting a fruit, like a lemon, with awareness and curiosity and see if this changes your assumptions or expectations.
- Being curious during meditation practice, for example noticing what happens when you observe a thought without entering into the full meaning of it.
- Bringing curiosity into your daily experience, like noticing sights and sounds around you with a sharper focus as you walk to work.

FEELINGS

Our normal, everyday state tends to be one of being caught-up in tasks, activities, unresolved problems, and so on, that spin around in a cloudy soup of wants, anxieties, tiredness and possibly stress. Of course, there may also be positive feelings and emotions as well. This draws our conscious energy and attention, not as we might like to think, into the objective outside world, but into a dynamically changing narrative of our situation, "The story of me" as it is today, bound together with thoughts and emotions.

The emotions we experience are a blend of feelings and thoughts. We can get a handle on thoughts; we can see or hear them running through our heads and most of them are accessible to conscious awareness.

When it comes to feelings, it's like visiting a different country, where we don't know the language. Feelings are not open to inspection; they can only be felt, acknowledged and interpreted with the mind. We know feelings are powerful, as they change our relationship with our experience, both positively and negatively.

Using a layered model of thoughts, emotions, feelings and sensations, we can say that feelings are sensations that have some form of meaning. We feel "butterflies in the stomach" because we're excited or anxious; tight and heavy muscles around our jaw because we're angry, or tightness and tension in our neck and shoulders when we're stressed. So, a good way to notice and acknowledge feelings is to be more aware of what's going on in your body in the present moment. You can then explore the actual sensations with curiosity as well as thoughts, to find out what the feeling is about.

For example, you may be walking down the street and notice that a negative feeling has crept in; for some reason, you're not feeling as good as when you left the house. Checking in with your body, you feel slightly heavy, a little bit low and there's some tension around your chest and shoulders. You even notice that your posture has dropped slightly. You then realise that you just went to the cashpoint and your current balance was much lower than expected. By acknowledging the feelings and sensations, relaxing your chest and shoulders, and possibly responding with the positive thought that you get paid in a few days, the feelings dissipate and dissolve by the time you get home.

We tend to notice feelings that are negative, limiting and depleting more easily than ones that are positive, expanding and nurturing. Working with negative feelings means embracing and acknowledging the sensations and thoughts so that they are allowed to dissolve. The good news is that when we really notice positive feelings, they sustain and expand. The important thing is to focus your attention on the actual sensations, rather than the thoughts about what triggered the positive feeling. This is different from our impulse to try and hold onto the source of positive feelings, which is about the future, rather than the actual experience in the moment.

As an example, you may notice a beautiful sunset on the horizon and feel a strong sense of peace, contentment and connection. Rather than having thoughts about not wanting the sun to disappear, simply connect with the positive feelings by bringing your attention and awareness to the physical sensations within your body, maybe feelings of lightness, tingling and flowing energy. You can try this out easily by taking a moment to appreciate a beautiful flower or plant that may be nearby.

The fact is that we experience more positive feelings than we acknowledge or appreciate. These range from the mundane, a good cup of coffee, or lying in a comfortable bed ready for a good night's sleep, to the cosmic, looking up and appreciating the stars in the visible universe. By working skilfully with negative feelings, we allow them to dissolve, and with positive feelings, we expand our experience of happiness and wellbeing.

~

SUGGESTED WEEKLY PRACTICE

- Get into the habit of checking what feeling tone is around during the day by asking "What's going on for me now?"
- Acknowledge and move towards feelings and see if you can allow them to dissolve in their own time rather than holding onto them.
- Notice the push and pull impulse towards the pleasant and unpleasant in your body and explore what happens when you create a bit of distance between who you are and these feelings.

FIVE STEPS

Every night we close our eyes and let go of everyday conscious awareness when we sleep. And every morning we wake with fully-formed thoughts, emotions, physical sensations, sounds and images that make sense to us. This process, which we've experienced every day of our lives, is one of those mundane, yet extraordinary things, that we hardly ever think about and often take for granted.

Most experts agree that consciousness has two parts: the background awareness and the foreground content. Although it's possible to be aware of both, we tend to mix one with the other, while focusing almost exclusively on the content.

Like particles in a shaken snow-globe that swirl around in the water, our attention gets bound to the content of consciousness; caught in its energy and momentum. And like fish, who apparently don't know they're in water, we're often blind to the broader background of awareness.

Given that our evolutionary advantage stems from being able

to understand, represent, process and communicate things and events in the world, our focus on content is not surprising. For instance, as hunter-gatherers we may have told the group where the ripe fruit was located.

Like the water in the ocean, apart from when we're asleep, conscious awareness is there all the time in the background, whether we notice it or not. On the other hand, the content of consciousness comes and goes; a thought emerges, is noticed and then dissolves. What's interesting is that when we get caught up in automatic thoughts, we lose awareness of the here-and-now and drift in a world of content, from one thought to another.

Some of the core mindfulness skills are about improving our attention and awareness. This includes noticing when we get caught up in content as well as becoming more familiar with the conscious awareness in the background of our experience.

One challenge with improving our awareness of mind-wandering, is that it's almost impossible to notice the transition. One moment we're happily walking along, fully aware of sounds, sensations and the movement of the body, and the next we've drifted off in thought about the meeting on Wednesday, or replaying that embarrassing event on holiday last summer. This is something we're all familiar with. One explanation of why noticing the transition is so difficult is that the brain automatically switches modes when our level of awareness drops and takes our attention with it. This is one of the primary ares that mindfulness works on - developing awareness and improving your attention skills

Here are five fundamental steps that underpin mindfulness practice that we'll return to again and again:

1. Noticing that your attention has wandered and that your awareness has dropped
2. Disengaging your attention from the automatic thoughts
3. Anchoring yourself back into the present by connecting with your breath, body and senses
4. Settling in the open, aware space and stillness that lies beyond content and movement
5. Then responding to whatever arises in the moment with open awareness, flexibility and kindness

You can use this process in any moment in your day to bring you back to a mindful and aware state.

These steps can also be used for embedding your formal mindfulness practice. For instance, this could be 10, 15, 20 or 30-minute sitting practice, where you first settle your body, mind and emotions and then work with whatever arises in your experience with the five steps. You can either move through the steps, or stay in a step to deepen the practice. For instance, anchoring your attention and awareness in the present with your breath, body and senses. And whenever your attention drifts, start with step one again. Beginning again as many times as it takes.

Mindfulness is not about stopping thoughts; it's about becoming more familiar with the awareness that rests peacefully in the background of experience and responding skilfully to whatever arises in the present moment.

SUGGESTED WEEKLY PRACTICE

- Remember to do your best to notice when your mind wanders during the week.
- Be kind with yourself and don't engage in self-critical thoughts.
- If you find your mind wandering, bring your attention to your body and senses, which are only ever in the present moment.

14

JUDGING MIND

Imagine that you're driving and come across a car in front crawling along and moving erratically. You immediately start making judgements about the driver's ability and begin to feel annoyed that they're in your way and holding you up when they shouldn't be on the road. You hoot loudly with annoyance and drive past, turning to frown at the driver as you pass. It's then you notice that the driver is an elderly woman and the car has a flat tyre.

When people are behind the wheel of a car they become even more judgemental than when they're walking. Research in the psychology of driving found that drivers dehumanise other drivers in ways they would never do when interacting with someone face-to-face. Similar behaviour also occurs online in social media.

We make judgements all the time, although there's a big difference between carefully considered, intentional judgment, like evaluating a business case, and the automatic running commentary of our experience that includes judgemental thoughts. Just think of all the things you like or don't like, label good or bad, or judge as pleasant or unpleasant.

We can be judgemental of others, ourselves, and things in the world, like a song, a film, or type of food. When judgement is turned inward, we're on the receiving end of our inner critic. One way of exploring this is to imagine that you have a smart speaker, like Amazon's Alexa, talking back to you with a critical running commentary, "*Why are you so useless? You're always late. No wonder people don't value what you say as you're unattractive and not likeable enough...*" This may sound laughable and we'd soon switch the unit off, but we sometimes entertain and identify with a similar internal dialogue inside our heads.

Automatic judgements impose limits on others and ourselves. When we judge other people, we separate ourselves and limit the other person, as they become little more than the judgement in our minds. Thoughts tend to overlay and filter the reality that's in front of us, whereas actual reality is always much more complex, interconnected and expansive than we think it is. The result is that automatic judgemental thoughts rarely serve us, or other people, well.

Evolutionary psychologists suggest that judgement was important for early humans, as they needed to know who they could trust, as well as understand their relative status within the group. Social comparison theory says that we constantly evaluate ourselves in relation to others, often in terms of attractiveness, wealth, intelligence and success. Social comparison plays a powerful role in influencing our opinions, beliefs and self-worth and is used very successfully in advertising, politics and the media. Most opinions, beliefs and prejudices originate from these areas and then become unconsciously embedded in how we evaluate the world.

Surrounded by these influences, it's no wonder that we form automatic habits with our judging mind.

So how can we break the habits of our judging mind?

Firstly, we can be more aware of judging thoughts as they arise. We can acknowledge the thoughts and then recognise the difference between thoughts and reality. If the judge-mental thought is about someone, instead of entertaining it, bring a sense of connection, kindness and compassion and notice how this changes your relationship with your experi-ence. And by the way, it's also important not to judge ourselves for having judgemental thoughts.

Our judging mind is deeply ingrained and operates when we wander off in thought. We're social animals so it's no surprise that we evaluate and compare ourselves with others. When the judgemental thoughts emerge automatically they're powerful because they're operating under the radar of our awareness, which is when the inner critic can do most damage. To break these habits and attachments, all you need to do is clearly observe the judging thoughts as they arise in awareness and cultivate an attitude of gentle non-judging. Over time this will bring clarity, insight, wisdom, connection and compassion to your relationship with yourself, as well as other people around you.

SUGGESTED WEEKLY PRACTICE

- Notice when you have judgemental thoughts and use curiosity to see where they come from.
- Observe to see if judgements are intentional, or do most arise from unintentional automatic thoughts?

- Watch out for self-judging thoughts that limit who you are. All you need to do is clearly observe them in open awareness, which shines a light on these old habits and significantly reduces their power.

15

LISTENING

M any of us take our ability to listen for granted. We listen to the sound of conversation, music, birdsong and traffic. Our ability to hear evolved over millions of years and goes all the way back to early fish who used a hair cell to detect changes in water pressure. Over time a series of special small bones evolved to form the inner ear that mammals, including humans, have today. For animals, ears are useful for sensing danger, communication and, in some cases, navigating the environment. The ear also provides an important sense of balance. Sound is a wave of vibrations that travel through the air or another medium. Humans can hear frequencies from 20 to 20,000 Hertz, or cycles per second, which varies by individual and declines with age. Some animals like dolphins and bats can hear up to 100,000 Hertz, while elephants can hear sounds as low as 14 Hertz.

Hearing is the raw sense of picking up sounds, while listening occurs when we make sense of and apply meaning as we perceive what we hear. As social animals, our ability to listen, understand and communicate is so important that the frequency range we hear may well have evolved to optimise around the sound of the human voice. So, we have this amazing sense of hearing combined with powerful processing in our brain, which helps us make sense of what we hear.

If only we could simply listen to what other people are saying. As we all know, simply listening can be a bit of a challenge. In a typical conversation, we may be listening to what someone is saying with "half an ear", while also getting drawn into our own internal dialogue. It's interesting that conscious thinking works by semi-verbalising in our own heads. For instance, asking, "Where did I put my keys?" causes related thoughts to emerge from memory. In the same way, when people talk through an anecdote, for example, travel problems on holiday, we'll experience similar anecdotes arising in our own mind. We then experience a strong impulse to share what's on our mind, before we forget and the conversation moves on. At other times we get so caught up in our own thoughts, we completely fail to hear what's being said. This is not helped by the fact that we can listen and process information much faster than someone can speak, which means we tend to anticipate and think ahead. On top of this, adding distracting technology like smartphones into the mix and it's no wonder that we sometimes feel ignored.

Listening mindfully means:

- Setting the intention to listen mindfully with open awareness and kindness
- Putting aside your inner dialogue and focusing your attention on the sound of the speaker's voice and words being said
- Giving your undivided attention - if your mind

wanders, bring your attention back to listening
mindfully
- Removing any obvious distractions like screens and
smartphones, if you need to communicate properly
- Being patient and allowing the other person to finish
what they're saying, without interrupting or jumping
to conclusions
- Using curiosity to really listen – as if your life
depended on it
- Not judging, or imposing limitations on the other
person – allowing them to be a full and complex
human being just like you
- Noticing your habits and impulses, for instance,
wanting to interrupt with your advice, or anecdote
- Acknowledging any insights or intuitions that emerge
through non-verbal communication, as well as your
own emotions, thoughts and physical sensations,
without being distracted by them

There are many benefits of listening mindfully: you build
better relationships by connecting with people and bring out
the best in them; people feel appreciated, so are happier and
more productive; people feel heard, so they work better
together, and with greater understanding the right things get
done.

SUGGESTED WEEKLY PRACTICE

- When listening to someone try focusing on the
sound of their voice and see what happens.
- Notice what's going on in your own mind when you

are listening. For instance, getting ready for what you want to say, rather than listening properly.

- See if you can let go of impatience when listening and bring kindness, openness and generosity to the other person.

❧ 16 ❧
NOTICING

Have you ever lost your keys in the house? You know you used them to open the front door, the phone was ringing and you remember sitting down and having a conversation. But now you need to go out again and the keys have disappeared. You must have put them down somewhere...

The chances are either you've done something like this, or know someone who does this kind of thing. When an important object like a set of keys, phone, or purse mysteriously vanishes, it was generally placed somewhere by someone who failed to notice what they were doing in the moment. We'd like to think that we're perceptive individuals and notice most things. The truth is that there are many subtle barriers to really noticing in the moment.

Noticing means to observe, take note of; to perceive. Noticing is where we choose to place our attention and connect attention with awareness. Noticing connects us with reality, which can lead to insight and understanding. When we really notice we become the witness of our experience.

So, what are the barriers to noticing? The first is that we're creatures of habit, some that serve us and some that don't. Habits are the embedded routines that operate outside our awareness. The human brain uses up to 20% of the body's total energy, using more energy than any other organ, so it makes sense to take short cuts: not fully processing the familiar, filtering out what's not important and using labels and assumptions. A good example is that our visual field is only really processed and focused around the centre, while everything else is relatively blurred in the periphery.

Another barrier is that our attention is easily distracted by the busy and noisy world around us, as well as our own mind-wandering thoughts. And thirdly, sometimes we just don't have the energy or capacity to really notice, owing to work overload, stress, lack of sleep or anxiety.

So how can we improve noticing as a skill? One answer is to bring curiosity and beginner's mind to our experience. Physicists say, "Reality is not what you think it is"; it's always richer and more complex, so there's always something to be curious about.

Beginner's mind means seeing things as if for the first time, rather than through the limiting labels and assumptions that overlay and filter reality. With greater openness, we are more open to possibilities, whether this is a situation or an individual. We can also make sure we have the energy and capacity to notice, by getting a good night's sleep, exercise and nutrition.

The things we notice do not need to be big and significant; sometimes they could be really mundane, like noticing a flowering weed growing out of the pavement.

Here are ten suggestions on things to notice:

1. Where your attention is
2. When your mind wanders and the thoughts you're having
3. Other people with openness and kindness
4. Your sense of connection with others
5. The world around you
6. The soundscape you are in
7. Physical sensations in your body
8. Feelings and emotions
9. The impulse to react, so you can respond skilfully instead
10. The sound of your own and other peoples' voices

So next time you mislay your keys or mobile, you can use it as a prompt to raise your game and actively notice your experience in the present moment.

SUGGESTED WEEKLY PRACTICE

- When you walk use curiosity to really notice what's going on around you. For example, the wild flower growing at the side of the pavement, the blackbird call in the trees, or the coolness of the air on your face.
- Try playing a game of labelling your experience; thinking, breathing, seeing, walking, as your attention shifts around and see how long you can keep it up.
- Use the times you put down daily objects like keys, phone, purse or wallet as a prompt to bring yourself into the aware and alert present.

❧ 17 ❧

ONE THING AT A TIME

In today's world of work, there's always more to do and fewer people to do it. So, we tend to work longer hours and try and pack more into each day. This leads us to juggle activities at the same time so we can complete what needs to be done. Of course, there are times when multi-tasking is useful and necessary. Sometimes we just need to get stuff done and the only productive way is doing more than one thing at a time. However, when we multitask we switch our attention between tasks, which research tells us can reduce productivity by up to 40%. Other research found that having our attention on social media while we work can lower our IQ by 10 points while we are on the task.

The habit of multitasking creeps into almost everything we do. The assumption almost seems to be that if you're not doing more than thing at a time, you're not working hard enough. But are we confusing quantity with quality? There are many important tasks that really require a high quality of sustained attention, combined with mental clarity. For instance, solving a complex technical issue, producing an important customer proposal, or planning a project.

Switching between tasks fragments our attention. We lose the thread, are more likely to make mistakes, are less productive and increase our level of stress. Working in a perpetual rush, we end up feeling frustrated and dissatisfied, rarely finding the quality time and space to complete work that we're proud of.

The various calls, messages and alerts that arise during the day are just the most obvious interruptions to our attention. With mindfulness, we learn to become much more aware of how our mind wanders and disconnects our attention from what we're doing. Our own wandering thoughts are the most powerful distraction of all and often the greatest challenge to maintaining focus on a task.

In mindfulness, doing one thing at a time is referred to as acting "one mindfully". This means if you are walking, rather than drifting off in thought, simply walking and opening your senses to the world around you. If you're having a conversation, rather than rehearsing your response, focus your attention on listening to what's being said, with kindness and curiosity.

As you experiment with focusing on one thing at a time, you'll soon notice that the habit of multi-tasking soon tries to take over and that it's surprisingly difficult. One useful tip is to focus on "where the work gets done". For instance, this could be where the knife peels the skin off the potato, where the brush touches the wall as you paint, where the text appears on the screen, or your fingers touch the keys, as you type. Another tip is to take a brief pause at the end of each task, before you consciously begin a new task; a simple mindful breath will do.

As well as practising the mindfulness skill of doing things "one mindfully", there is a range of practical things you can try to break the multitasking habit when you really need to focus.

- Shut down email and go back to it towards the end of the day
- Switch off notifications on Smartphones, tablets and computers
- Set your instant messaging app to "Do not disturb"
- If you really need peace and quiet, find somewhere quiet, or see if you can work from home when no one else is around

Whatever you want to achieve, you'll be more successful if you maintain mental focus and clarity. People sometimes defend multitasking as the only way to get things done in a busy world, which may work for some simple tasks, but not when things are more complex. Building the habit of doing one thing at a time may seem counter-intuitive, but in the end, it's a real time saver and will boost your productivity.

We're bombarded by all kinds of distractions, including having our attention high-jacked by our own wandering mind. Doing things "one mindfully" has many other benefits, including connecting you into the present moment with what you're doing, which can make even peeling potatoes a surprising pleasure.

∾

SUGGESTED WEEKLY PRACTICE

- Bring one thing at a time into domestic tasks like

washing up, peeling potatoes, or cleaning the bath and see what difference it makes.

- Notice what happens when you multitask. Do you actually get more done to a higher level of quality?
- Set a few rules on distractions during the week, like only doing emails at the start and towards the end of the day, not taking your laptop into meetings, or leaving your mobile outside the bedroom and see what happens.

18

PATIENCE

If you drive, you've probably experienced waiting at a traffic light, not moving off the millisecond the lights change and being hooted at by the impatient driver behind. For whatever reason, the driver cannot wait and we're in their way. We share this planet with 7.7 billion other people, so we all have to wait at some point; waiting for the train, at the dentist, or the supermarket checkout. The trouble is, the world we live in today is built around pace, meeting deadlines and getting things done. In fact, research on Internet speeds shows that people start to lose patience after as little as a two-second delay. Living at a faster pace may mean we get more done, but when we're forced to wait, we can become irritated, frustrated and even anxious, which builds up tension and stress in our body.

Patience is the ability to accept having to wait, be delayed or face setbacks without reacting. This means being more aware of what's going on and working skilfully with thoughts and emotions that arise in our present-moment experience. If we're unaware, our options are limited, so we're more likely to react automatically. Practising patience is often a more skilful response.

So why is it that we find waiting such an unpleasant experience? The simple answer is that we've not learned to practise a deeper level of patience. Impatience is our mind's way of leaning into the future; getting to the next moment, as if that moment is somehow more important and meaningful than our experience now. Impatience is a form of aversion, a desire to get rid of something. It's also about resisting our experience, as we feel uncomfortable in the here and now.

As well as waiting, we can also feel impatient when we're working on something, driven by anxiety about the need for completing whatever it is, rather than accepting and enjoying the on-going process. Our intolerance of accepting delay is an indicator of our tendency to live in a projected future in our heads.

So how can we cultivate patience?

Here are some tips on improving patience as a skill:

- Be more aware of situations that test your patience, notice feelings and thoughts of discomfort, irritation, annoyance or anger before they really take hold, using curiosity to explore the emotions and physical sensations you're experiencing.
- Use each situation where you feel impatient as an opportunity to practise patience and see what difference that makes
- Is the situation really intolerable? Are you making exaggerated assumptions about how unpleasant the situation really is? When you are in the situation that challenges your patience, take a moment to really explore how uncomfortable it really is. Is this more

about delaying you from future moments? Are the future moments any different from your present experience?

- Become more aware of the tendency of your attention to drift off in thought, imagining what you may be doing in a future moment, rather than connecting with your actual lived experience in the present
- Pause, take a deep breath, accept the reality of the situation and open your awareness to the surprisingly rich experience that this moment holds

Mindfulness is about working skilfully with your present-moment experience. Patience is one of these skills that can be learned and developed. When we're impatient we can experience anxiety, anger, and stress, which are not skilful.

By developing patience, we also cultivate other skills of acceptance, openness, awareness and kindness, and when we practise patience, we reduce anxiety, anger, and stress and improve our relationships. So, by practising patience we move towards an easier and healthier life.

SUGGESTED WEEKLY PRACTICE

- Notice when you feel impatient during the week and instead bring patience.
- Be curious about the situations that make you feel impatient.
- Be aware of the habitual impulse to want to get to the next moment, as this one is unsatisfying and not good enough.

19

PEACE

There are special moments in our lives when we found peace: really letting go and relaxing on holiday or stopping for a few moments to admire the view when walking in the countryside. We often strive to find a bit of peace, where we experience a deep, harmonious alignment with the world around us at that moment. The trouble is, in the world today, with all its turbulence, noise and uncertainty, peace is often difficult to find.

We can pick up disturbance every time we watch, read or listen to the news, which often demonstrates that there is little peace in the world, with wars, wildfires, violence and political and economic disorder. Using the latest technology, huge amounts of information is filtered, condensed, prioritised and presented in the news. And just in case you might have missed something, some news channels have a newsreader competing with other news scrolling and flashing on the screen as well. It was not always this way. Although it's some time ago, there was a famous BBC news broadcast in 1930 where the news announcement was, "Good evening.

Today is Good Friday. There is no news", as it was decided that nothing newsworthy had happened. They played piano music instead.

So, is there peace underneath all the turbulence and noise in the world?

We often think of the world that includes smartphones, cars, coffee bars, financial services, holiday adverts, airports, super-markets, and motorways as part of the same world that includes nature, but they're not the same. What if we sepa-rated out the "world": everything that humans have created, from the "earth"; the blue planet seen from space, nature itself? Using this distinction, it's easier to see the world as a man-made overlay. Although it's governed by the laws of nature, it tends to be a lot more chaotic; always in a state of flux, uncertainty, and disturbance. So, although we may not be able to find much peace in the world, we can find peace when we connect with the earth through nature.

Although there is sometimes conflict in nature, for instance, a volcanic eruption, most of the time there is peace and harmony. Think about the last time you walked through a woodland. There were the trees, the sound of a wood pigeon and sunlight glinting through the leaves in the upper branches. Apart from the changing seasons, nothing much was happening. The earth is always in relative harmony and peace is abundant. Caught up in the busy content and activity in the world, it's hard to find peace. It's when we drop beneath this noisy overlay, into a more natural space, that we find true peace.

Suggestions for finding peace include:

- Settling agitation and letting go of holding onto emotions, stress, tension, and tightness

- Reconnecting with nature – earth rather than the world
- Taking an occasional digital detox for half a day, a full day or a weekend
- Practising acceptance, rather than avoidance or resistance
- Avoiding getting pulled into the news for a day or two and see what difference this makes
- Connecting with space, stillness, and silence that rests in the background of experience, rather than the foreground objects and content that we normally inhabit

They say, "Rest in peace" when someone dies, but we all aspire to find a bit of peace and happiness while we're still vibrant and alive. Trying to find peace at work and in our personal lives is a real challenge. By looking in the right places and moving towards peace in nature we may uncover the peace inside ourselves.

Suggested weekly practice

- See if you can find time at the beginning of each day to find a little bit of peace.
- Avoid getting into conflicts or arguments before bed time, protecting the peaceful hours before you go to sleep is a good idea
- If you need a bit of peace, take a deep breath and sound the word "Peace" internally as you slowly exhale allowing mental agitation and noise to dissolve as you imagine a clear open sky.

20

PRESENCE

In today's world we've become used to filling up all the precious moments of our lives and rarely experience a few quiet moments of simply being, without something to distract us. It's as if we've become unconsciously obsessive and anxious with the need to fill up any empty space and still-ness in our experience with more content and activity. We've developed many ways of making sure we remain busy, with 24-hour news, social media, chat, email, TV, smartphones, radio, newspapers, and so on. We're almost constantly engaged in content; forgetting what it's like to do nothing for a few moments, and even feeling a bit guilty if we stop.

For tens of thousands of years of human evolution there was more time to relax and fewer distractions, so it was probably much easier to watch the sun rise, listen to birdsong or lie back and enjoy the clouds drifting across the sky. Today, many of us can't even go for a walk without being distracted; over the last few years there's been a rise in pedestrian accidents, as more people slowly walk along, immersed in their smartphones. And of course, we're also distracted by the thoughts running through our heads, which is another form of virtual reality that adds to our inability to simply be with the present moment as it is.

The polar opposite of all this outer and inner distraction is presence; the alert awareness, aliveness and openness to present-moment experience that is beyond thinking. Presence is available in every moment and is something everyone can access. Even in our most stressed, anxious, or low moments, the inner resource of presence lies quietly in the background of our experience. Presence is being calm, relaxed and open, where we experience a natural state of connected wholeness and wellbeing.

We've all noticed the profound experience of presence at some point in our lives. Maybe a peaceful moment on a mountain, looking at a sunrise over the ocean, or walking quietly in the woods. But if presence is intrinsic to human experience, we can't rely on having to go to these special places to experience it. And if presence is so important, why do we fail to notice it?

Like a ticking clock, presence becomes subsumed into the unnoticed and unacknowledged background of our experience, as the brain filters it out. We tend not to notice what's going on in the background as our attention is drawn towards foreground activity and content. We tend to think that mundane everyday tasks like cleaning our teeth, or taking a shower are boring, so our attention automatically switches to more interesting things, like drifting off in thought about the day ahead. Neuroscientists have discovered that there's actually a part of the brain, called the default mode network, which hijacks our attention into mind-wandering when it seems that there's nothing much going on.

In our modern lives, we don't make it easy for ourselves to experience presence. Cultivating presence is something we have to work on, by bringing our attention away from thought and into the calm and alert awareness, aliveness and openness to the moment- to- moment flow of experience.

Presence is also about:

- Exploring our sense of aliveness, aware of the moving energy and sensations around the whole of the body from the inside out.
- Coming to our senses and resting in the space and stillness behind sounds and movement. Allowing and remaining open to whatever arises in our awareness.
- Noticing and acknowledging sensations, feelings and thoughts as they arise, play out and pass away.

Rather than being completely immersed in the foreground content, movement and noise of experience, which comes and goes, we can rest in the background of presence, our unwavering home and refuge, where we can access and express our full potential. Presence is also a source of creativity, clarity and wisdom and has the power to transform our experience in all areas of our lives.

$\sim$

SUGGESTED WEEKLY PRACTICE

- Notice what takes you away from presence. Is it busyness, your smartphone, the habit of mind-wandering?
- If you feel a bit stressed, negative and limited try

coming into the present by connecting with you body and senses.

- When you are out in nature, like walking in the woods, take a moment to stop and really breath in and appreciate the peace and presence that's already there.

21

REACTING AND RESPONDING

Reacting and responding are similar words, but they mean subtly different things. If we have an infection, we hope that our body responds to the antibiotics rather than reacts to it. Like a carpenter working with the grain, rather than against it, mindfulness is about working skilfully with present-moment experience. This means creating the mental and emotional space to respond skilfully to whatever arises, rather than reacting automatically, which can often make a difficult situation worse, or add friction to our relationship with others.

Like the saying, "knee-jerk reaction", when we're stressed or agitated we often react without examining the facts, before we know what actually happened. At times of stress we can switch into fight-or-flight mode, which has limited access to inner resources, like the ability to properly assess a situation, review options or think clearly.

Of course, there are times when physically reacting fast can be useful and even save your life, for instance when you hit the brake as a car suddenly swerves into your lane. This type of reaction is driven by the brainstem, which keeps us alive, but is not the sort of reaction we're talking about here.

When we react there is no pause between the event and the reaction; no space to reflect; no flexibility; no choice. Viktor Frankl, the neurologist, psychiatrist, author and Holocaust survivor said, "Between stimulus and response there is a space. In that space lies the freedom and power to choose our response. In our response lies our growth and happiness".

Responding is about being in a calm, balanced and alert state, where you have the internal capacity to assess a situation, review options and select the most appropriate response.

Here are some tips on responding rather than reacting:

- How you respond is something you control; reacting is something that controls you
- Try not to personalise, as the event or situation might have occurred whether you existed or not
- Realise that there are always choices and options
- Pause and take an aware breath. For instance, when your phone rings, let it ring three times while you bring yourself into the moment
- Practise allowing and accepting, working with the grain, without avoiding or resisting reality
- When you do find yourself reacting, as we all do at some point, try to really observe what happened and see if this provides insights and ideas on what you could have done differently
- Ask yourself "am I reacting? "

Responding blends bottom-up emotion and top-down think-ing. A skilful response is informed by our knowledge and experience of the situation, but also includes the awareness of our own and other people's emotions

By practising mindfulness we learn to become more aware of our internal states, which allows us to shift from the limitations of an agitated, restless state into one that's more expansive, calm, open and alert. This creates the space for responding skilfully to whatever arises in our experience, which, as Viktor Frankl said, leads to growth and happiness.

SUGGESTED WEEKLY PRACTICE

- Notice when you to tend to react automatically, is this with particular people? Is it a bit of an unconscious habit?
- Be more aware of the impulse to react and realise that there are always other options.
- If you find yourself reacting, bring kindness to yourself and others and learning from the experience.

22

RECLAIM YOUR ATTENTION

Y ou may have heard of the non-violent, direct-action collective called "Reclaim the Streets." During the 1990s this group took over a section of road so that pedestrians, rather than cars, have priority for the day, by reclaiming and opening up public space. We can look at our attention in a similar way. Attention is one of the most precious resources that is, theoretically, within our direct control for the whole of our waking life. In practice, our attention is conditional on how aware and awake we are in any particular moment.

Not only do we have our own internal challenges with automatic thoughts at the edge of our conscious awareness; we're also surrounded by technology, media and content that's designed to attract and grab our attention. Every time we post, share, or like, we set up the expectation of a social reward, which triggers a little dopamine high, a neurotransmitter involved in the experience of reward and pleasure. Social media and gaming companies have been developing smarter ways of gaining our attention for years and they're now very good at it. This challenges the attention skills of the generation who've grown up with social media; they can become addicted to these platforms, are prone to distractions and develop short attention spans.

It's ironic that when humanity faces complex global problems like climate crisis, economic instability and over-population that our ability to focus our attention has never been more challenged.

On a personal level, we need to be the master of our attention, rather than its servant. The addictive, dopamine high that's being triggered by social media and gaming tends to reward the passive, rather than the active, intentional direction of attention. Imagine that you're in a darkroom, but have a torch. If conscious awareness is the torch light, attention is where the torch is directed. Attention can be focused and narrow, like when writing an email, or broad and open, for example when driving on a motorway. We can also focus on inner experience like thoughts, emotions and physical sensations, or through our senses, to notice what's going on in our environment.

From when we're born, our brains adapt and become wired to learn about and interpret the world we focus on; we literally become what we pay attention to. With mindfulness practice, we get better at noticing where our attention is over the day. For instance, sometimes our attention will be focused on the task, then thinking about the meeting tomorrow, then vaguely drifting on nothing in particular.

When we practise meditation, we can notice how fast our attention switches from say, focusing on the breath one moment, to running through a shopping list for dinner, the next. Without warning, our attention can shift with the speed of a fast edit in an action movie. One indicator is that our attention is more likely to be distracted when our level of awareness drops and part of the brain involved in automatic thoughts, called the default mode network, takes over.

Reclaiming our attention and building our attention "muscle" is essential for mindfulness. Observing the breath, noticing that our attention has drifted off in thought and bringing it back to the breath is a foundational practice of mindfulness meditation. We can also practise both focused and open attention, which also helps build our attention skills.

Mindfulness is about working skilfully with present-moment experience; to do this successfully we need to know where our attention is. If you accept that the present-moment is the only time we can experience being alive; if our attention is distracted somewhere else, are we really fully alive in that moment?

SUGGESTED WEEKLY PRACTICE

- Notice where your attention is by asking "Where is my attention now?" snd see what insights emerge.
- Be curious about the things that tend to distract your attention and use the simple breathing practice to build your attention muscle.
- Acknowledge and appreciate that we are not always masters of our own attention, but there are things we can do to improve our focus.

❦ 23 ❦

SENSATIONS

M ost of us are brought up to believe that the ability to think is the most important thing. We spend years in formal education developing our minds and building knowledge, but hardly any time, in most cases literally no time at all, learning what it really means to be human. As well as thoughts, we all know we have emotions, feelings, and sensations, but are not taught what these really are or how to work with them effectively.

Sensations can be external and internal, so include all the senses as well as the physical sensations in the body. Sensations are the low-level signals that arise from the body and senses before they are interpreted and made sense of by the mind, which is the process of perception. So, for hearing, the sensation would be the raw sound of a bird call and the perception would be that it's a magpie. Physical sensations are part of the somatosensory nervous system which extends throughout the body and includes skin, muscles, bones, joints, the cardiovascular system and internal organs

From a young age, we realise that our body is relatively independent from the world around us, as we develop an individual identity based on our body – a sense of "me". Although we may have been curious about our body when we were children, our relationship with our body tends to change dramatically when we reach adolescence. We then typically become overly self-conscious about how we look in a superficial comparison with our peer group and what's considered attractive at the time, in our society. And as we get older, apart from health issues, aches or pains, our body seems to slip into the unconscious background of our experience, numb and hardly noticed.

One useful way of thinking about the relationship of sensations to our experience is to view sensations, feelings, emotions and thoughts as layers.

Thoughts
Emotions
Feelings
Sensations

- Thoughts are at the top and are abstract and conscious
- Emotions are a blend of feelings and semi-conscious thoughts
- Feelings are sensations that have some meaning
- Sensations are at the bottom and are tangible and relatively unconscious.

Sensations can drive feelings, emotions and thoughts from the bottom-up. Thoughts can drive emotions, feelings and sensations from the top-down. Of course, this is just a way of making sense of the relationship between these elements; in reality they blend into one another and are part of the same whole, open system.

Interestingly it's these same levels that developed over millions of years of evolution, from reptiles, mammals to humans that have resulted in how the human brain is wired.

The point of exploring thoughts, emotions, feelings and sensations in this way is that it:

- Brings neglected areas of the body into conscious awareness
- Connects us with the direct experience of being alive in the present moment
- Helps us become whole and complete
- Allows us to make better use of, and work more skilfully with, these amazing natural resources that make us human
- Brings greater appreciation together with a sense of awe and gratitude about what it means to be alive

Mindfulness encourages us to take a break from living all our lives in the noisy and sometimes cramped city of the mind, to explore the broader landscape of emotions, feelings and sensations that are also all part of what it means to be human.

~

SUGGESTED WEEKLY PRACTICE

- Reconnect and build a closer relationship with your own body and sensations.
- Notice the feelings beneath emotions and the sensations beneath feelings.

- Acknowledge and appreciate the pleasure and aliveness that we experience through sensations.

SENSES

Even before we enter the world as babies, we're already responding to sensory experience, like sounds for instance. As we develop and become adults, what we receive through our senses becomes part of the background of experience we take for granted, until we discover we have a problem, like noticing that the book we're reading is at the end of our arm. Of course, there are also times when we really appreciate our senses, like the taste of an amazing meal or the beauty of the tree blossom in the park.

We get used to the five primary senses of sight, hearing, taste, touch, and smell, but there are other senses that are now included by science. Some of these tend to be unconscious and subsumed into everyday life. Where your sense of touch ends at the surface of your skin, the interoceptive sense tells you about what's going on inside your body. This includes whether you're hot or cold, tired or hungry. There's also the kinaesthetic sense that tells you where your body and limbs are at any time, for example, when you duck your head to enter a low doorway. Dancers and athletes have a more refined and conscious kinaesthetic sense. We also tend to think of our senses as the physical sense organs like our eyes or ears, although large parts of the brain are also involved in making sense of the world around us.

The senses in our head are directly connected to the brain in various ways; for instance, vision through the retina at the back of each eye, smell through the olfactory lobes above the nasal cavity and sound by the auditory nerve to the brainstem. There are specialist areas of the brain involved in processing sensory input, like the visual cortex for instance, and other areas that combine inputs from different senses to give us a joined-up view of the world. Our brain uses the rich combination of senses to make sense of the world, which includes filtering out input that's not worth processing, as well as information that conflicts with a joined-up experience.

There's a difference between raw sense and perception. For instance, the eye has a blind spot where the optic nerve passes through the back of the eye, but processing in the visual cortex completes the gap for us. Another is that the image on our retina at the back of the eye is always upside down, but our brain turns the image the right way up for us.

Vision is the dominant sense for humans, which uses up to forty percent of our cerebral cortex. In contrast, touch uses around eight and hearing just three percent. Our dominant visual processing is one reason good practice in communication includes advice like, "a picture paints a thousand words" and "show, don't tell".

Directly connecting with our senses is an important part of cultivating mindfulness. Coming to your senses directly connects you into the present flow of experience, away from automatic thoughts that previously grabbed your attention. We can use skills like curiosity and "beginner's mind", as if freshly experiencing things for the first time, to break out of the limiting assumptions we hold about the world around us.

And we can explore the five external senses, as well as internal senses, to really appreciate the everyday miracle of what it means to be alive. We tend to make assumptions about our senses, for instance, that there's nothing more to explore. But what does it mean to really see a landscape like an artist; to taste an organic tomato like a food connoisseur; to smell a rose like a perfumer?

Although most of us are fortunate enough to have a full range of working senses, how much do we really appreciate and feel gratitude for what our senses provide? When you think about it, apart from thoughts, the majority of our experience comes through our senses. And even thoughts can be in sound and images, they use the same parts of the brain as those involved in sensory processing.

There is only this passing moment of experience. We can only fully appreciate the rich aliveness and beauty of the world around us, in all its wonder, when we intentionally come to our senses.

Suggested weekly practice

- Notice as many senses as you can when you go for a walk, the sounds, sights, smells, touch as well as the sense of your body in movement.
- Do things that expand and stretch your senses. For instance, eating a piece of fruit and appreciating a

whole range of flavours, textures and sensations, or hearing a sound that you consider noise and finding harmonic tones within it.

- Really appreciate and feel gratitude for the senses you have.

❧ 25 ☙
THINKING

We all know that thoughts are powerful; they help us solve problems, inform important decisions, guide us to act, make sense of the world and provide new ideas and possibilities. Collectively, thoughts helped us land on the moon, invent the Internet and control much of the world around us. Less positively, collective thinking has also led to conflict, prejudice and the destruction of the environment.

Given that thoughts are so important, what are they and how did humans develop the capacity to think in the first place? The challenge with answering the first question is that the brain is the most complex phenomenon known to humankind. Although there's been significant progress in the brain sciences, we actually know much more about the visible universe than what goes on inside our own heads. The subject is complex, as thoughts emerge in the typical adult brain with around 100 billion neurons across 100 trillion synaptic connections. By comparison, there are an estimated 100 billion galaxies, similar to our own Milky Way, in the known universe.

According to Wikipedia, although there are many theories, there's no generally accepted view on what a thought is, or how it's created. The same goes for how symbolic language evolved, with little agreement among scientists and academics. The most recent research by archaeologists and anthropologists in Africa studying early hominid engravings estimate that symbolic thinking evolved something like 70,000 years ago, which means that our species, Homo sapiens, already had the ability to think when it emerged around 10,000 years later.

As far as we know, although mammals can access memory and experience emotions, they do not have symbolic thinking, so live in the moment. Before the development of language, early humans probably had a similar experience. It's interesting that the development of secular mindfulness is often about letting go of thinking and coming back to the body and senses; as if we've gone too far in our minds and need to recover some balance.

You may have come across the simple three-brain model of brain evolution: The brain stem, or reptilian brain, provides all the vital functions to keep us alive, followed by the mammalian or emotional brain and on top of this is the neocortex, or thinking brain. Humans have all three stacked on top of one another. Luckily for us, part of our brain is nearly always connected in the moment, even though our attention may be somewhere else. While we drive down a motorway, off in thought, other parts keep us safe on the road.

Protected by our skull, our brain knows nothing about the world, apart from what it perceives through the senses. As it develops, our brain builds and adapts an internal model of the world, which we construct and change over a lifetime. Equivalent to "you are what you eat", our mind becomes what we feed it, whether this is daytime TV, trashy social media, inspiring conversations, or a good book.

Recent research has found many linkages between thinking and physiology. One of the best-known is the power of placebos in medicine. When people are given painkillers without any trace of the drug, their brains release endorphins, which reduces pain. Given how the neocortex is connected to the lower parts of the brain and body by the autonomic nervous system, it's no surprise that our state of mind can affect our heart rate, breathing and immune system. So our state of mind can make us physically Ill, as well as healthy and full of vitality.

Now that psychology and neuroscience have a better understanding of the mind and brain, we realise that we over--identify and lack awareness of our thoughts, which allows our mind to become our master rather than our servant. Practising mindfulness helps us change this relationship and make better use of our mind, by becoming more aware of thoughts and disengaging from automatically identifying with them; leading to a healthier, happier and more productive life.

Suggested Weekly practice

- Becoming aware of dominant habitual patterns of thought that no longer serve you.
- Encouraging expansive, positive and nurturing thoughts and paying less attention to limiting, negative, depleting thoughts .
- Knowing that you are not your thoughts; being able to discriminate between reality and how your mind interprets the world.

26

TRUST

D riving on the motorway at seventy miles an hour in the middle lane, you are overtaking slower vehicles on one side and cars are speeding past on the other. You feel relaxed, listening to the radio, thinking about plans for the weekend. All of this is possible because you've placed your trust in the other drivers, in the manufacturer of your car and the organisation that maintains the road. You may even trust your Sat Nav. As an alternative, you could travel by train, but then you're still trusting the train driver and the railway operating company. When you think about it, our society would break down immediately if we could not trust one another; social trust is the glue that binds everything together.

Some people find it easier to trust other people than others, which often links back to differences in parental attachment during childhood. Someone with a difficult upbringing may not automatically trust people in the same way as an individual who experienced a safe and secure childhood. Our general level of trust in people can also be damaged in adulthood, if we suffer painful relationships, or are let down by others. On top of this, social trust is also under threat in the fast-moving society we live in. For instance, for many people, the use of misinformation, or "fake news", as it's sometimes called, has eroded trust in politicians and the media.

For tens of thousands of years, our ancestors evolved in small social groups, where everyone saw each other as relatively equal, in a trusted and supportive community. Although this sounds idealistic, this is backed up by anthropologists studying hunter-gatherer tribes today, who found many interesting behaviours that we could learn from.

We now live in much larger and complex societies. In a big city, we're often surrounded by complete strangers, whom we've never met and are unlikely to ever see again, which would cause our ancestors enormous stress. So, it's no surprise that people in cities tend to filter-out the built-in need for social connection, almost seeing other people as cardboard cut-outs.

With mindful awareness, we can override this tendency by being more conscious of social trust and actively trusting most people we encounter. Of course, this means being wise and skilful, rather than naïve. Using open awareness and kindness, we can see other people as being just like ourselves, with joys, challenges and a complex inner life just like our own. You can practise this while commuting and at work. For instance, say you're introduced to new people in a meeting at work, notice if you begin not trusting people you don't already know as a default behaviour. If you discover that you're not automatically trusting someone at work, it could be that there's something about the way they come across, or that you're projecting a lack of trust onto them; if this is the former, you may be right not to trust them. If the latter, it's likely that you work in an environment where trust has been eroded, which is common in organisations that have an endemic blame culture.

There's also an individual level of trust, in ourselves. Every day we trust that our bodies function properly; we trust our breath and heartbeat, that our lungs extract oxygen, neurons fire, gut bacteria work away, cells are replenished, and we see, hear, smell, taste, and touch. It's not that we have a choice, but we put our faith and trust in all these wonderful things.

Also, rather than sometimes looking outside for guidance, we can also trust that we have the right inner resources, knowledge and experience, insights and intuition; trusting that if we are aware, calm and alert, we'll respond skilfully to whatever arises in our experience.

Practising mindfulness means taking responsibility for being our authentic self, learning to listen to and trust our inner responses and aware sense of being. And as we cultivate trust within ourselves, we'll find it easier to trust other people; appreciating the basic goodness in everyone.

SUGGESTED WEEKLY PRACTICE

- Appreciate the trust that we have in other people who help us on a daily basis.
- Trusting in your own insight and intuition of what you observe in awareness.
- Bringing openness and kindness to others as we realise that they have a complex inner life just like our own.

27

WHY MEDITATE?

As human beings living in the 21st Century, we have access to some amazing technology and previously unimaginable amounts of information. Yet many of us work in organisations where doing more with fewer people has become the norm. Although we do our best to manage the tsunami of tasks and demands, we can easily end up feeling stressed, anxious, agitated and overloaded. In this state, we're more prone to being distracted by automatic thoughts as well as reacting automatically, which limits and degrades our performance and wellbeing.

When we meditate we reverse this momentum, slowing down the whirlwind of activity to access a gentler, more aware, peaceful and expansive sense of who we are. Rather than being lost in thought about the past or future, we're anchored in the present moment; appreciating and aware of our body and senses; re-connecting with the peace, stillness and potential that's always available behind every moment of experience.

Meditation has been practised for thousands of years and can be found in all major religions. There are many different types: watching the breath, listening to an internal repeated sound, chanting and inner contemplation, among others.

Within mindfulness there are generally two types: focused and open. Focused concentration helps build the attention skills and develop concentration and awareness of present-moment experience. The intention is to hold your attention on an object like the breath, physical sensations or sound and bring it back to the object if your attention is drawn away with a distraction. Focusing one-mindfully, on one thing at a time, is an example of using this skill informally during the day. Open monitoring meditation is about being open to whatever arises in your experience, whether this is a thought, emotion, feeling, sensation, or sense perception. Whatever arises, the content is noticed in open, expansive awareness without reacting, grasping, resisting, avoiding, liking or not liking. Whatever arises is allowed to play-out and release back into the natural background of experience. An example of informal open monitoring during the day is to notice and allow whatever arises on a walk, for example.

We often use both of these forms of meditation, although open monitoring is seen as a more advanced practice that becomes easier with consistent focused attention practice. Regular meditation trains our attention and expands our awareness. It also helps create the space to think clearly, respond more skilfully, be more creative, notice more, and access useful insight and intuition.

No one is ever a perfect meditator: everyone experiences difficulties with meditation at some point. Our minds will always wander. Although automatic thoughts can be useful, providing solutions to difficult problems, insightful and creative, they can also be limiting, depleting and negative. By practising mindfulness meditation, we're able to notice when this happens and experience fewer negative automatic thoughts. Apart from eating healthily, regular exercise and getting enough sleep, neuroscientists found that regular meditation practice contributes to brain health and performance, including improving memory and learning.

Some meditation tips include:

- Before you start each meditation set an intention and attitude for how you are going to dedicate this time
- Like brushing your teeth, you'll experience much greater benefits if you manage to weave consistent practice into your daily routine. After a while, you'll not feel ready for the day without it
- People have been doing this for thousands of years and all of them got better with consistent practice
- Meditate somewhere that's comfortable, where you'll not be disturbed
- If you're pressed for time, it's better to meditate for 2-3 minutes than none at all
- If you have thoughts and anxieties about keeping time, try using a mobile phone app like Insight Timer
- Be kind and gentle with yourself and let go of any self-criticism about difficulties with your meditation – it's not a competitive sport
- The goal is not to stop or block thought. One of the key skills is to notice, as soon as you can, when you have gone off in thought, then gently bring your attention back to the object of the exercise.

Whatever your reasons for cultivating mindfulness, whether to reduce stress, anxiety, low mood, or improve performance, relationships, creativity or general wellbeing; you will experience a faster and more noticeable impact, by establishing a daily meditation routine.

Suggested weekly practice

- Experiment with meditating for ten to fifteen minutes in the morning for a couple of days, followed by a day without, and see what difference that makes.
- Our minds will always wander, so don't get to critical if sometimes you find that you've been off in thought rather than meditating.
- Noticing that your mind has wandered is actually a significant step. There are millions of people who have no idea that this is what happens to their attention.

28

WORKING SKILFULLY

Mindfulness is about working skilfully with whatever arises in your present-moment experience. Working skilfully means bringing the right skills and attitudes to your experience. Although we tend to think of the past, present and future as a continuum that we could potentially access, the reality is that it's only ever now; the flowing moment of experience. We can explore thoughts about the past through our memory and have thoughts that anticipate the future. Sometimes these are about "thinking on purpose", for instance planning a holiday, and at other times we automatically drift off in thought when our minds wander.

In theory we all have the capacity and opportunity to work skilfully with each passing moment. The reality is that we are often not as skilful as we could be. There are a number of obstacles that make this difficult:

- The first is that we may not be as aware and awake as we could be, so the moment passes us by.
- When we're under stress or are not fully aware, we

tend to react automatically with past habits and behaviour patterns, rather than responding skilfully.

- These ways of coping can also lead us to avoid or resist anything that appears as a threat, or is seen as unpleasant, in our experience.
- And to complicate matters even further, we tend to automatically identify with our thoughts and emotions, which gives them a power they may not deserve. For instance, we may momentarily lose our phone and in the panic say to ourselves, "Why am I so stupid?" Although this is just a thought, without awareness this can end up diminishing our self-worth.

So what are some of the mindfulness skills and attitudes that can help overcome these obstacles and allow you to work more skilfully with your experience?

- The most obvious one is that you're awake and aware of what's going on in the present. Ways to improve this include getting a good night's sleep, eating healthily, exercising and practising mindfulness during the day. This could be a simple ten-minute breathing practice at the beginning of the day, walking mindfully, or listening to a guided meditation on the train into work.
- You can make sure you're grounded in the present by connecting with your body and senses, which are only ever in the here-and-now.
- Noticing automatic patterns of behaviour can help you change automatic reactions that are no longer useful. Simply observe what happened when you reacted automatically, with open awareness, kindness and curiosity and take note of any insights.

- Also noticing your tendency to avoid or resist some things and instead bring the attitude of openness and acceptance to the reality of a situation.
- Creating a bit of space and separation between your thoughts and feelings and who you are means you're less likely to react and automatically identify with thoughts and feelings. Although they're both really useful, thoughts are just mental content and emotions are just energy flowing through you. Also, by creating space you have better access to inner resources, including a choice of options for how you can respond more skilfully.
- Working skilfully with emotions as they arise, acknowledging what you're feeling and allowing them be just as they are, so they can play out and dissolve naturally, rather than kept alive for much longer with thoughts about the emotion. Researchers in this area estimated that a typical instance of anger lasts only 45 seconds, if left to run its natural course.

Of course we all work with what arises in our experience; sometimes more skilfully than others. The only time we have any real freedom and flexibility to make a difference is in the present moment, which is where cultivating mindfulness makes a real difference; reducing stress, anxiety and low-mood, improving communication and relationships and helping you live life with greater ease.

~

Suggested weekly practice

- Appreciate the benefits of working skilfully in terms

of wellbeing as well as performance at work and in your relationships.

- Congratulate yourself every time you manage to respond skilfully rather than react automatically during the week.
- Use curiosity to notice the link between being present and the ability to work skilfully.

29

GUIDED PRACTICES

The guided audio practices are available to play or download by registering at:

https://www.mindfulcall.co.uk/kgyfxc/

By completing this simple form, you'll be added to the mailing list for book updates and also be able to access all the guided audio practices that support this book. When you register you will be sent to the guided practices page. Make sure that you bookmark this page, or add a shortcut to your smartphone for future reference.

During each session, you can either sit on a chair or on the floor. However, you sit, if it's comfortable for you, see if you can maintain a relatively upright back with your head balanced at the top of your spine, as this allows you to stay more alert and for energy to flow.

When you're comfortable and ready:

- Play the brief settling practice for the session, closing

your eyes, or gently lowering your gaze as you follow the guided practice

- Then open your eyes and read the session chapter at your own pace
- When you're ready, play the theme-based guided practice as you close your eyes
- As the session comes to an end, maybe read trough the suggested weekly practice and set the intention to include this into your week

If you get an opportunity, perhaps reminding yourself during the week about the theme and listening to the theme-based practice again.

To experience real benefits from mindfulness, it's important to not just do the formal practice, like the meditations, but weave the practice into your day and week, which is one of the things this book has been designed for.

So, if it works for you, it's recommended to begin each day with a minimum of five or ten-minutes sitting practice. For instance, this could be a simple focus of attention on your breath and body, with your eyes closed, as you travel into work on the train.

Hope you found this book and the supporting guided audio practices interesting and useful . If have a moment to spare, I would really appreciate a short review on Amazon, as this helps new readers find my books. Also, feel free to share on social media to help spread the message about mindfulness.

Thanks and best wishes

Paul

ALSO BY PAUL RICHES

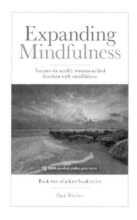

Available on Amazon in eBook and print formats

ABOUT THE AUTHOR

Paul Riches has been teaching mindfulness in the work setting since 2012 in
large organisations, including BT plc
and Transport for London and has
helped thousands of people experience
the benefits of mindfulness.

Paul first encountered meditation and awareness exercises
when he went through a difficult time in his early twenties
and found that the practice made a real difference to his
happiness and well-being.

He has a BSc in Cognitive Science and an MBA. He has
trained in Mindfulness-based Cognitive Therapy and follows
the Good Practice Guidelines of the UK Network for Mindfulness-Based Teachers.

For more information
www.mindfulcall.co.uk
paul.riches@mindfulcall.co.uk

Printed in Poland
by Amazon Fulfillment
Poland Sp. z o.o., Wrocław

54661560R00066